# Cross-Stitch
# MANDALAS

## 20 Unique Projects Celebrating Color Stories from Around the World

### ISABELLE HACCOURT VAUTIER

## STACKPOLE
## BOOKS
Essex, Connecticut
Blue Ridge Summit, Pennsylvania

T0357818

# Preface

In this book, I wanted to take on a design—the mandala—that I find very specific and interesting in current visual arts, partly because of its spiritual and therapeutic aspects.

"Mandala" is a term borrowed from Sanskrit (India), meaning "circle," "sphere," "environment," and "community." It is used in Hinduism, Buddhism, and Jainism, with "manda" meaning "essence" and "la" meaning "container."

Drawing or coloring mandalas can reduce the level of stress and anxiety that many of us experience and soothe the mind, either through the concentration it requires or through the colors chosen. As I designed and colored mandalas, I wanted to find out more about the colors I was drawn to and what my choice of colors was trying to tell me or make me think about, and sometimes, to what places those colors brought me.

I found myself researching sometimes unfamiliar countries, just because the colors or the design I had drawn took me to this or that place. I also tested my inclinations on those around me by asking them which country my drawing and colors reminded them of, and often we were very close on the destination.

I studied and read a lot about the benefits of color therapy (chromotherapy) because I believe it is beneficial. I also believe, even more so, in the benefits of crystal healing (lithotherapy), which is complementary to it.

There are in fact six main colors in Buddhist religious texts, five of which, excluding black, represent the five personifications of Buddha. These five colors are also present in nature, and here are their meanings:

– White: purity and emancipation

– Yellow: humility and renunciation

– Red: luck, passion, and fulfillment

– Blue: healing, wisdom, and life

– Green: balance and harmony

– Black: shadow and ignorance

If I were to add my own perceptions to this symbolism, after finishing this book, I would add that white represents for me all that is dream, the beyond, the breath of life; yellow is cheerfulness, warmth, well-being, and protection; red is passion but also anger, fire, heat, and blood ties; blue is peace, calm, water, serenity, and freedom; green is nature and thought; and black is the forbidden, silence, and secrecy.

Everyone has a very different vision of colors, and this can be seen in what you wear or choose for your home.

It's my esoteric side, I think, that invites you to take a journey through these pages, so that I can share with you a little bit of this road that is both colorful and zen. You're free, of course, to change the colors of your cross-stitch as well as your fabric choice and frame or how you use it. These choices will take you on faraway travels, perhaps alongside me or to a country other than the one I've described.

Fasten your seatbelts! The journey begins now. Wishing you all wonderful, colorful cross-stitches!

**Isabelle Haccourt Vautier**

# Contents

# Resources

**ISABELLE HACCOURT VAUTIER**
*https://www.creationsisahv.com*
*https://www.creationsisahv.fr*
*e-mail: isavautier@wanadoo.fr*

**DELPHINE VASSEUR, TAKALFAIRE**
*https://couleurs-cabanes.fr*
*Facebook: takalfaire*

**AUVERGNE LASER 63**
*https://www.al63.fr*

**THIEFFRY FRÈRES**
*https://www.thieffryfreres.fr*

**ZWEIGART**
*https://shop.zweigart.de*

**DMC**
*https://www.dmc.com/US/en*

**LORNA BATEMAN EMBROIDERY**
*https://www.lornabatemanembroidery.com*

**MILL HILL**
*http://millhillbeads.com/index2.php*

---

*Information on the properties of crystals/stones should not be understood as medical advice. Consult your health care practitioner for medical diagnosis and treatment.*

# Bulgaria

Occupying the central part of the Balkan Peninsula, modern-day Bulgaria is in a territory with a complex history, where great civilizations have crossed paths and come into conflict with each other for thousands of years.

A natural crossroads between Europe and Asia, the Balkan Peninsula has always been an important communication route, both for mass migrations and waves of conquest.

The colors I have chosen for this design are bright springtime hues. The predominant pink symbolizes romance, tenderness, and softness. Strange as it may seem to us, in the Middle Ages, pinkish red was the symbol of virility for men. It was only later, with the romanticism of the eighteenth century, that pink became a symbol of femininity.

ASSOCIATED STONE

## Rhodochrosite

### *Benefits*

<u>Mental</u>

✳ Boosts creativity and inspiration for musical compositions.

✳ Acts positively on memory.

✳ Heals emotional and romantic wounds.

✳ Promotes feelings of love and compassion.

<u>Physical</u>

✳ Acts positively on the nervous system.

✳ Soothes ulcers and arthritis.

✳ May help stabilize certain forms of diabetes.

✳ Acts on certain heart problems and palpitations.

✳ Has beneficial effects on the skin.

# Bulgaria

## DIMENSIONS

Stitch count: 108 x 108
7 x 7 in. (18 x 18 cm)
for the center of the tea
towel

3.9 x 3.9 in. (9.8 x 9.8
cm) for the pincushion

## SUPPLIES

• Thieffry Frères Ecru/
Fuchsia tea towel with
center in 16-count aida
cloth (6 st/cm)

or

• Zweigart 27-count Black
Linda evenweave (ref.
1235, color 720) (11 thr/
cm) for the pincushion

• DMC Mouliné Embroidery
Floss: 600, 904, 907,
3609, 3804, 3806

## INSTRUCTIONS

Center the pattern on the
fabric you have chosen.

For the tea towel, cross-
stitch using 2 strands of
embroidery floss.

For the pincushion,
embroider using 1 strand
of floss over 1 thread of
the fabric.

| X | DMC |
|---|-----|
| ⋒ | 600 |
| ⋏ | 904 |
| S | 907 |
| ✕ | 3609 |
| ▼ | 3804 |
| ◉ | 3806 |

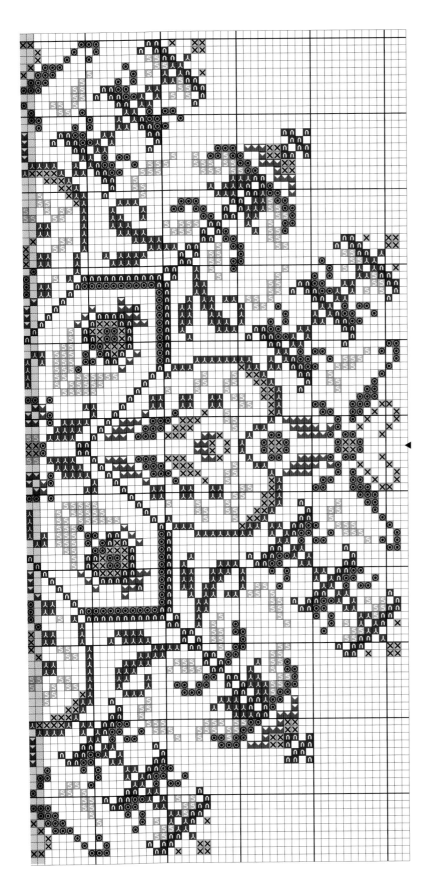

Attach the black fabric to a
wood pincushion base from
Lorna Bateman Embroidery.

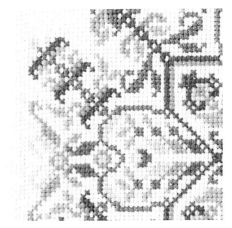

7

# Moscow

I initially drew this pattern directly on the screen, just letting my imagination run wild, and then searched for the destination to which it was leading me. When I put the design on a black background and saw it along with the colors and the shape, it became obvious that Moscow was the place. At the time I drew the design, Moscow was not embroiled in international conflict, so I left Moscow as I dreamt of it, for its rich art and architecture.

I then tried to get as close as possible to the colors of traditional costumes, adding a touch of "Snow Queen" blue. This specific blue, slightly opalescent and milky, ends up being predominant.

There is a distinction between the light blues (associated with health, healing, wisdom, faith, and serenity) and the dark blues (associated, like black, with power, intelligence, and expertise).

Blue is also the favorite color of the vast majority of people around the world. Reassuring and soothing, blue is a positive hue that, depending on one's temperament, is most often associated with the ocean or the sky.

ASSOCIATED STONE

## Chalcedony

### *Benefits*

#### *Mental*

✳ Promotes creativity and self-expression in its broadest scope. It is the stone for artists and introverts.

✳ Alleviates sadness and anger. Brings peace and serenity.

✳ Facilitates communication, reduces shyness and tendencies toward verbal aggression.

#### *Physical*

✳ Soothes sore throats, stuttering, and hoarseness.

✳ Relaxes the larynx and eases tension or strain in the throat and vocal cords. Excellent stone for singers and orators.

✳ Accelerates bone repair.

# Moscow

## DIMENSIONS

STITCH COUNT: 57 x 183
4 x 13 IN. (10.3 x 33.2 CM)

## SUPPLIES

• ZWEIGART 27-COUNT BLACK LINDA EVENWEAVE
(REF. 1235, COLOR 720) (11 THR/CM)
• DMC MOULINÉ EMBROIDERY FLOSS:
16, 209, 211, 703, 725, 806, 827, 904, 3804

## INSTRUCTIONS

Center the pattern on the fabric and
cross-stitch using 2 strands of floss
over 2 threads of the fabric.

*I embroidered beads
onto the design for
a special touch.*

| X | DMC |
|---|---|
| ✖ | 16 |
| ▲ | 209 |
| C | 211 |
| ◀ | 703 |
| Y | 725 |
| N | 806 |
| ◉ | 827 |
| 3 | 904 |
| ▽ | 3804 |

# Bora Bora

**B**ora Bora is a small island in the South Pacific northwest of Tahiti in French Polynesia, surrounded by sandy islets called "motus" and turquoise waters protected by a coral reef.

This glittery turquoise fabric plunged me directly into the deep blue of Bora Bora. I set off on a journey imagining the great white sand beaches, coconut palms, and me, emerging from a beachside hut, happy to go off and embroider under the sun, sipping a colorful island cocktail. I know, I digress. But this place really makes me dream, so much so that it took

me practically the same amount of time as a plane trip from Paris to Bora Bora to draw my enormous pincushion design! I invite you to join this wonderful journey in embroidery if, like me, you don't have the financial means to actually travel that far.

The turquoise blue color is reminiscent of clear lagoon water. Refreshing and invigorating, this color inspires change, renewal, development, and transformation. It evokes youth, adolescence, escape, or travel.

The matching tablecloth is available as an embroidery chart in my online store.

ASSOCIATED STONE

## Turquoise

### *Benefits*

*Mental*

✳ Absorbs adverse energy and negative thoughts.

✳ Encourages positive thoughts and optimism.

✳ Promotes better social relationships and friendships.

✳ Boosts creativity and the development of one's potential.

✳ Alleviates depressive syndromes, edginess, and panic attacks.

*Physical*

✳ Boosts the immune system.

✳ Promotes healing of some injuries, such as ligament or tendon tears.

✳ Reduces eye infections.

✳ Detoxifies cases of poisoning and viral or bacterial infections.

# Bora Bora

## DIMENSIONS

Stitch count: 109 x 109
8.5 x 8.5 in. (21.8 x 21.8 cm)

## SUPPLIES

• Zweigart 25-count Pacific Metallic Blue Lugana cotton evenweave (ref. 3835, color 6136) (10 thr/cm)
• DMC Mouliné embroidery floss: white, 743, 820, 995, 3811, 3844, 3846

## INSTRUCTIONS

Center the pattern on the fabric and cross-stitch using 2 strands of floss over 2 threads of the fabric.

*Sewn by designer Delphine Vasseur ("Takalfaire," couleurs-cabanes.fr).*

| X | DMC |
|---|---|
| ● | White |
| = | 743 |
| S | 820 |
| ∩ | 995 |
| Y | 3811 |
| ◄ | 3844 |
| ε | 3846 |

15

# Botswana

**B**otswana lies to the north of South Africa between Namibia and Zimbabwe. It boasts a variety of wildlife habitats including the Okavango Delta, the Kalahari Desert, grassland, and savannah. Three-fourths of the country's inhabitants live in the southeast part of the country. There are very few large urban areas in Botswana, and they are of little tourist interest, so why did my design take me there?

I researched at length on the internet and in books to find where my imagination had led me, and Botswana fit perfectly with the colors I had chosen. I have never been to Africa and yet, there is some indefinable *je ne sais quoi* in African culture, look, music, and mystique that has always attracted and moved me.

Red being the dominant color, it first evoked warmth. In color therapy, red is usually associated with the first chakra, the root chakra, more traditionally known as Muladhara.

Red is also associated with fire; it stimulates passion and courage. It also promotes perseverance and endurance. Red is a color that warms hearts and awakens passion. It is the color of women, action, willpower, and leadership.

ASSOCIATED STONE

## Red Jasper

### *Benefits*

*Mental*

✳ Instills strength and dynamism to overcome apprehensions and doubts.

✳ Drives out the negative and stimulates the fulfillment of projects by supporting faltering determination.

*Physical*

✳ Possesses healing properties that can also correct certain irritations.

✳ Activates blood circulation and digestive functions and balances hormonal secretions.

✳ Provides relief during feminine sensitive periods such as pregnancy or menopause.

# Botswana

## DIMENSIONS

Pincushion stitch count: 92 x 66
7.2 x 5.2 in. (18.4 x 13.2 cm)
Pouch stitch count: 126 x 208
9.9 x 16.4 in. (25.2 x 41.6 cm)

## SUPPLIES

• Zweigart 25-count Red Lugana
evenweave (ref. 3835, color 954)
(10 thr/cm)
• DMC Mouliné embroidery floss:
white, 310, 725, 741, 906, 907, 995

## INSTRUCTIONS

Center each pattern on the fabric
and cross-stitch using 2 strands of
embroidery floss over 2 threads of
the fabric.

For the pouch, only half the chart
is shown. Turn it over to embroider
the second part symmetrically.

Pincushion

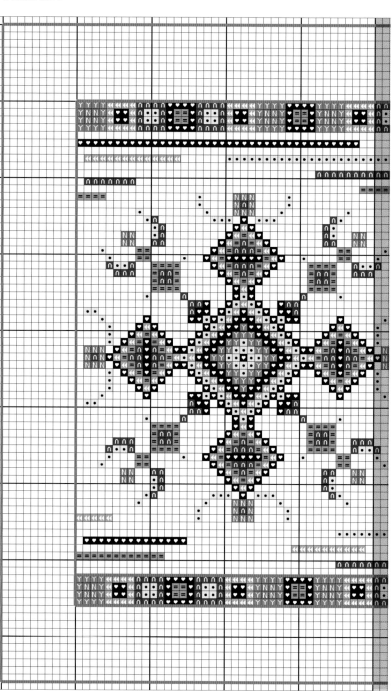

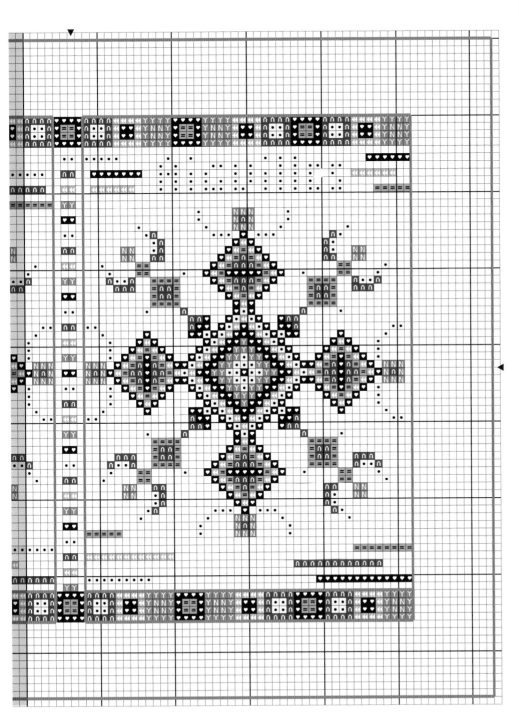

| X | DMC |
|---|---|
| • | White |
| ♥ | 310 |
| = | 725 |
| Y | 741 |
| N | 906 |
| ◄ | 907 |
| ∩ | 995 |
| — | Template |

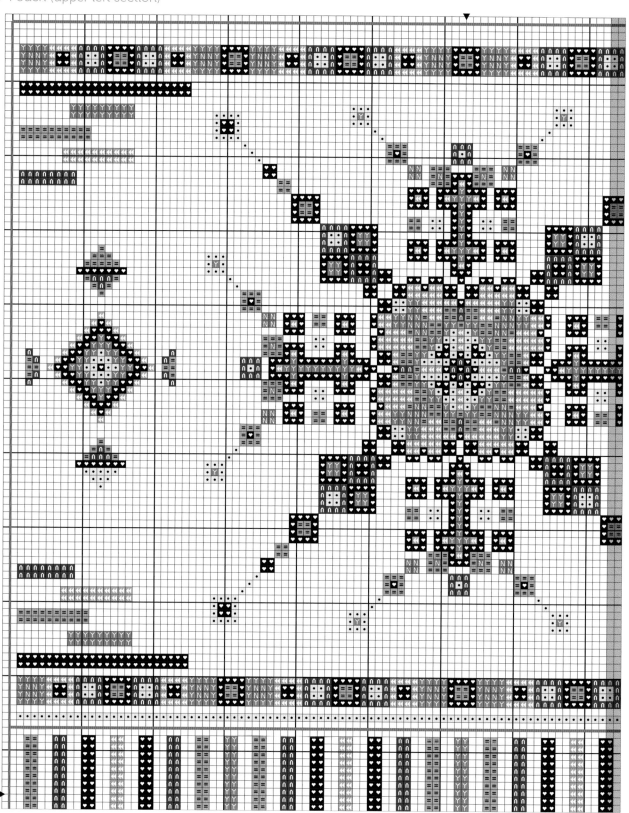

| X | DMC |
|---|---|
| ● | White |
| ♥ | 310 |
| = | 725 |
| Y | 741 |
| N | 906 |
| « | 907 |
| ∩ | 995 |
| — | Template |

# Pondicherry

This pattern is one of my treasures. I love it so much, to the point of having added a few sequins and beads to make it just a little more ornate without overdoing it.

Pondicherry, a city in southern India, was a trading post for almost three hundred years (1674–1954). The architecture of its streets, its diverse neighborhoods with their own particular characteristics (French or Tamil styles, sometimes a mix of both), its colors, its hidden gardens, its calm old French quarter and its friendly Tamil town, its human scale where you can walk or bike everywhere, its cosmopolitanism and religious tolerance, and its waterfront where everyone gathers morning and evening all give the city of Pondicherry a charm unique in India.

Saffron symbolizes attaining the happiness of a better state beyond renunciation, visible in the saffron-colored clothing that has always been reserved for Buddhist monks, emperors, and brides. A Hindu bride is ritually sprinkled with saffron by the women of her family before the wedding ceremony.

Magic attributes to saffron the powers of fertility, virility, and happiness, as well as psychic abilities.

*ASSOCIATED STONE*

## Citrine

### *Benefits*

#### *Mental*

✳ Fights depression.

✳ Eases digestion.

✳ Increases self-confidence.

✳ Reduces feelings of anger.

✳ Brings generosity and success.

✳ Combats stress.

✳ Strengthens determination.

#### *Physical*

✳ Benefits the heart and blood circulation.

✳ Positively affects the functioning of the thyroid gland, pancreas, intestines, and kidneys.

✳ Boosts metabolism and brings energy and vigor to the body.

✳ Regenerates tissues, accelerating natural self-healing processes through vibrations.

✳ Serves as a natural morning pick-me-up due to its light yellow color. It strengthens openness, supports, and brings a zest for life.

✳ Possesses strong energy. Protects against nightmares and brings restful sleep.

✳ Offers uses as a meditation stone.

This is a stone I am particularly fond of, and I have been wearing it on a ring since my grandmother passed away in 2007. It has a power that I can't explain, just like this Pondicherry pattern, which I am convinced has a very positive, indefinable *je ne sais quoi*.

# Pondicherry

## DIMENSIONS

Stitch count: 119 x 119
5.2 x 5.2 in. (13.3 x 13.3 cm)

## SUPPLIES

• Zweigart 27-count Black Linda evenweave
(ref. 1235, color 720) (11 thr/cm)
• DMC Mouliné embroidery floss: 612, 725,
740, 741, 900, 904, 905, 907, 3032

## INSTRUCTIONS

Center the pattern on the fabric and
cross-stitch using 1 strand of floss
over 1 thread of the fabric.

*Liven it up with some sequins or beads from
Mill Hill.*

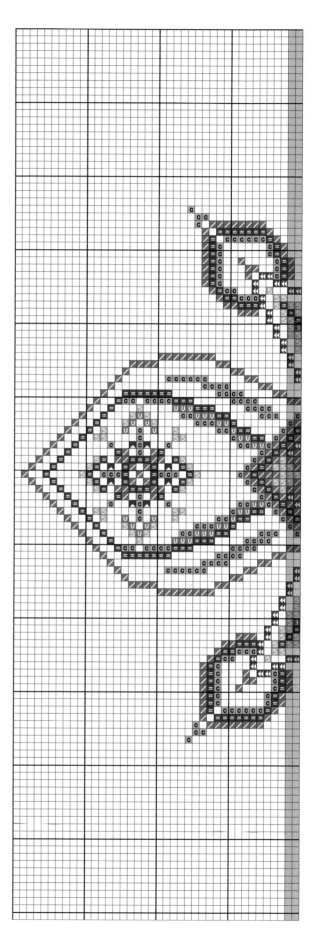

| X | DMC |
|---|---|
| ⁄ | 612 |
| C | 725 |
| U | 740 |
| Y | 741 |
| ═ | 900 |
| ▲ | 904 |
| ◄ | 905 |
| S | 907 |
| 3 | 3032 |

# Santorini

This destination is on my bucket list. I drew this design while looking at photos taken by my brother on one of his trips, which made me dream of this particularly wonderful place. This Greek island in the Cyclades, also known as Thera in Greek, offers magical views with intense contrasts. The whitewashed villages of the caldera stand against the black earth and the natural, rough volcanic sculptures.

The island of Santorini has been immortalized by countless poets and painters for its unique light, its colorful cliffs, and the breathtaking sunsets. This is one of the most beautiful Greek islands in the world that I hope, from the bottom of my heart, to be able to visit one day.

The dominant color is blue, reminiscent of the sea, but there is also a luminous white.

White symbolizes virginity, innocence, purity, and simplicity, as well as knowledge. It also represents strength, light, wisdom, and the divine. In some religions, white represents purification and absolution of guilt. If we think of marriage with the famous white wedding dress, this color can also signify the absence of failings, as well as fidelity.

ASSOCIATED STONE

## Rock Crystal (Quartz)

### Benefits

#### Mental

✳ Symbolizes purity, and more specifically, spiritual purity.

✳ Particularly suitable for meditation and concentration.

✳ Promotes expression and articulation and makes one more sensitive to the social and natural environment.

✳ Captures disruptive energies and promotes calm and harmony when placed in living areas and workplaces.

✳ Helps to relieve stress with its luminous energy.

#### Physical

✳ Brings vitality and comfort.

✳ Unlocks and channels energies and eliminates negativity.

# Santorini

## DIMENSIONS

STITCH COUNT: 147 x 147
9.2 x 9.2 IN. (23.3 x 23.3 CM)

## SUPPLIES

• ZWEIGART 32-COUNT CHARCOAL GREY BELFAST LINEN
(REF. 3609, COLOR 7026) (12 THR/CM)
• DMC MOULINÉ EMBROIDERY FLOSS:
WHITE, 162, 798, 799, 820, 3843, 3846

## INSTRUCTIONS

Center the pattern on the fabric and cross-stitch using 2 strands of floss over 2 threads of the fabric.

Then make French knots or replace them instead with Mill Hill Crystal beads.

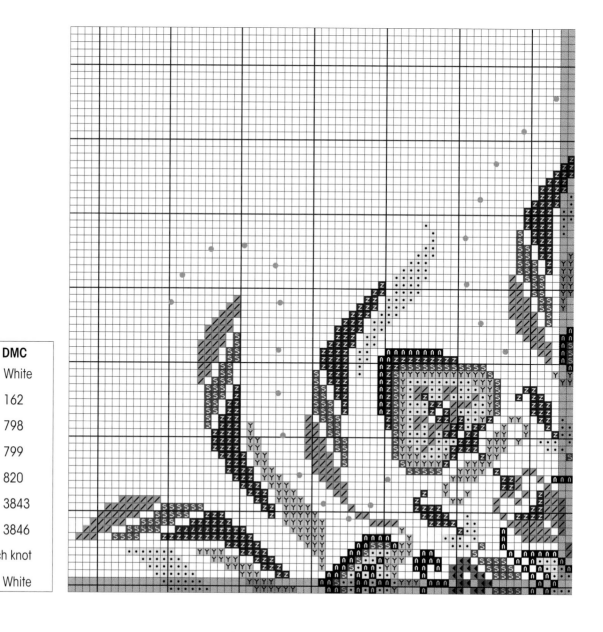

| X | DMC |
|---|---|
| • | White |
| Y | 162 |
| Z | 798 |
| ◀ | 799 |
| n | 820 |
| S | 3843 |
| / | 3846 |
| French knot | |
| ● | White |

Embroidered fabric made into a messenger bag by designer Delphine Vasseur ("Takalfaire," couleurs-cabanes.fr).

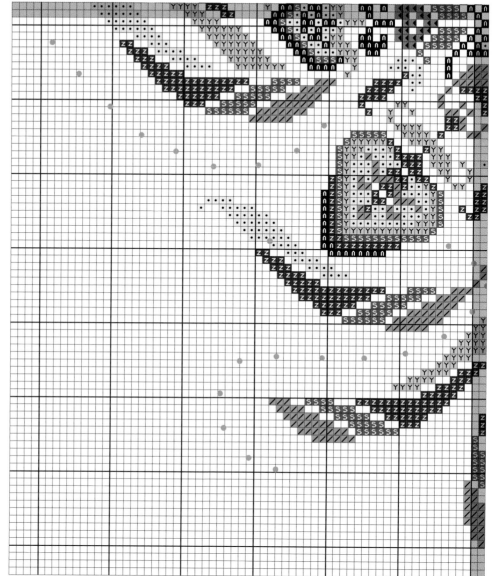

| X | DMC |
|---|---|
| • | White |
| Y | 162 |
| Z | 798 |
| ◀ | 799 |
| ∩ | 820 |
| S | 3843 |
| ╱ | 3846 |

French knot

| ● | White |
|---|---|

# Helsinki

The capital of Finland, Helsinki is enchanting, and its mandala quietly reminds me of the soft hues of its seaside landscapes, its world-famous architecture and design, and its delicious Nordic gastronomy, hence the idea for this table topper or overlay.

Nightlife in Helsinki is extremely active, with concert halls for alternative music fans and bars with live music where heavy metal bands play almost every night of the week. Every year, Helsinki hosts one of Europe's most significant metal/rock music festivals, featuring the current most popular bands from all over the world.

According to Wassily Kandinsky, a Russian abstract painter, "Blue is essentially a celestial color. The ultimate feeling it creates is that of rest." In feng shui, blue is the color of the soul and of wisdom. It represents tranquility. It also encourages reflection and meditation.

ASSOCIATED STONE

## Aquamarine

### *Benefits*

*Mental*

✳ Relaxes and quiets the mind.

✳ Strengthens budding love (especially when worn on an engagement ring).

✳ Calms anxiety and reduces nerves and emotional stress.

✳ Helps to find inner peace.

✳ Increases sense of responsibility.

✳ Develops tenderness and tolerance.

*Physical*

✳ Strengthens the immune system.

✳ Regulates the heartbeat.

✳ Soothes eyestrain.

✳ Combats motion sickness, particularly seasickness.

# Helsinki

## DIMENSIONS

Stitch count of Center Motif: 191 x 191
11.9 x 11.9 in. (30.3 x 30.3 cm)
Stitch count of corner pattern: 67 x 67
4.2 x 4.2 in. (10.6 x 10.6 cm)

## SUPPLIES

• Zweigart 32-count Off-white Murano evenweave (ref. 3984, color 101) (12 thr/cm)

• DMC Mouliné embroidery floss: 304, 352, 470, 472, 598, 726, 937, 3808, 3810

| X | DMC |
|---|-----|
| Ɛ | 304 |
| Y | 352 |
| S | 470 |
| C | 472 |
| X | 598 |
| ▼ | 726 |
| U | 937 |
| ∕ | 3808 |
| ⊙ | 3810 |

# Helsinki

## INSTRUCTIONS

Center the center motif on the fabric and cross-stitch using 2 strands of floss over 2 threads of the fabric.

Embroider the corner pattern in the 4 corners of the cloth at the desired distance from the center pattern.

Corner pattern

| X | DMC |
|---|---|
| Ɛ | 304 |
| Y | 352 |
| S | 470 |
| C | 472 |
| X | 598 |
| ▼ | 726 |
| U | 937 |
| ╱ | 3808 |
| O | 3810 |

# Osaka

Osaka is Japan's third-largest city. Located on a bay, it is the financial capital of its prefecture on the main island of Honshu. Osaka is renowned for its gastronomy, for being a hotspot of anime/manga activities, and for its dialect specific to the Kansai region.

Few know, however, that it is home to the first Buddhist temple built in Japan by order of the emperor.

I associate it with a dark violet to pink color, reminiscent of the hues of the sakura or cherry blossom flowers I love so much.

Purple has always symbolized the spirit, spirituality, and religion. In color psychology, mauve is linked to purple and thus to the themes expressed by this shade. Purple symbolizes protection, honesty, guidance, and the quest for meaning.

Violet suggests delicacy, gentleness, and dreams. It points to magic, fantasy, and imagination. This color conveys values of serenity and spirituality and can be associated with prosperity and nobility.

ASSOCIATED STONE

## Amethyst

### Benefits

*Mental*

✳ Soothing and purifying, reduces stress, calms insomnia, and promotes concentration and meditation.

✳ Helps find balance and serenity. Leonardo da Vinci wrote that it has the power to "dispel evil thoughts and sharpen the intellect."

*Physical*

✳ Favorable for falling asleep. If you have trouble getting to sleep or suffer from insomnia or restless nights, place an amethyst under your pillow for a peaceful night's sleep.

This stone is magical, and my teenager has one. It is a basic healing crystal to wear daily.

# Osaka

## DIMENSIONS

Stitch count: 111 x 112
6.9 x 7 in. (17.6 x 17.7 cm)

## SUPPLIES

• Zweigart 32-count Lilac Murano evenweave (ref. 3984, color 558) (12 thr/cm)
• DMC Mouliné embroidery floss: white, 209, 211, 327, 3346, 3348, 3804

## INSTRUCTIONS

Center the pattern on the fabric and cross-stitch using 2 strands of floss over 2 threads of the fabric.

Then make French knots or add Mill Hill Crystal beads.

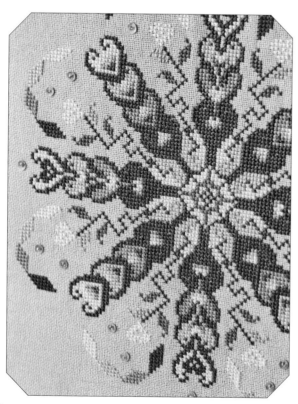

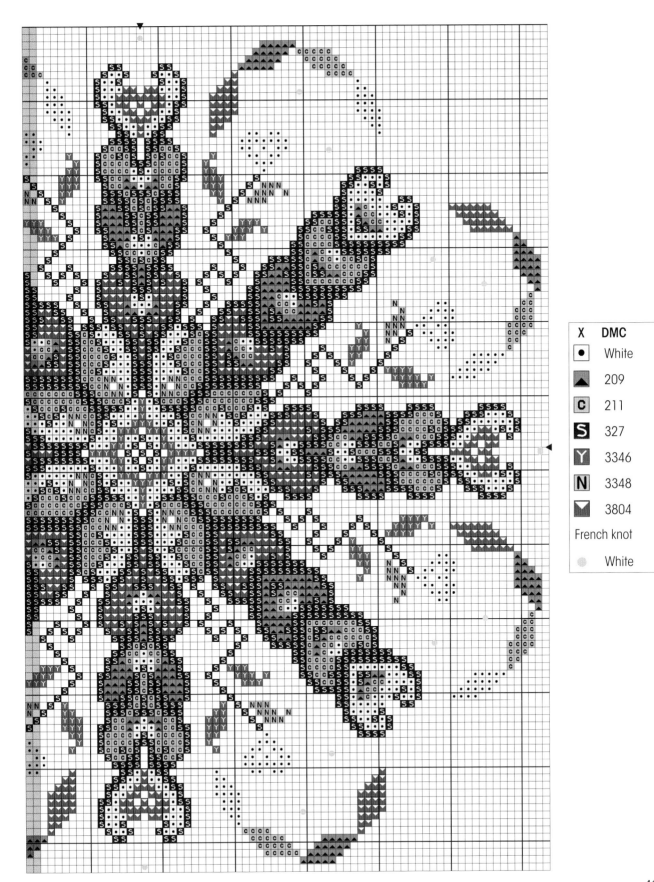

| X | DMC |
|---|---|
| ● | White |
| ▲ | 209 |
| C | 211 |
| S | 327 |
| Y | 3346 |
| N | 3348 |
| ▼ | 3804 |
| French knot | |
| ● | White |

# The Sahara

The Sahara, in northern Africa, is the world's largest desert (over 3 million square miles/8 million km²), which is why I chose a shiny, coppery color fabric. This vast, hot region extends over ten countries: Tunisia, Algeria, Morocco, Libya, Egypt, Sudan, Chad, Niger, Mali, and Mauritania. The temperature can get as high as 130°F (55°C).

Ochre, with either yellow or green dominant, is neutral or intermediate, the natural earthy color of soil, of humus at rest. Ochre is also the color of inner cheerfulness, not effusive, but happiness appreciated for its serenity and calmness. It is associated with a composed and thoughtful energy and reasonable, good advice.

ASSOCIATED STONE

## Tiger's Eye

### *Benefits*

*Mental*

✳ Promotes concentration.

✳ Stimulates attention.

✳ Fights fears and shyness.

✳ Increases self-confidence and willpower.

✳ Prevents lack of discernment.

✳ Reduces emotional blockages.

*Physical*

✳ Relieves joint pain and fractures.

✳ Facilitates walking.

✳ Fights hemorrhoids.

✳ Resolves biliary and nervous disorders.

✳ Combats stress.

# The Sahara

## DIMENSIONS

Stitch count: 53 x 53 (each design)
3.3 x 3.3 in. (8.4 x 8.4 cm)

## SUPPLIES

• Zweigart 32-count Shiny Copper Belfast linen (ref. 3609, color 3131) (12 thr/cm)
• DMC Mouliné embroidery floss: white, 310, 726, 817, 904, 907, 959

## INSTRUCTIONS

Center each pattern on the fabric and cross-stitch using 2 strands of embroidery floss and backstitch using 1 strand of embroidery floss over 2 threads of the fabric.

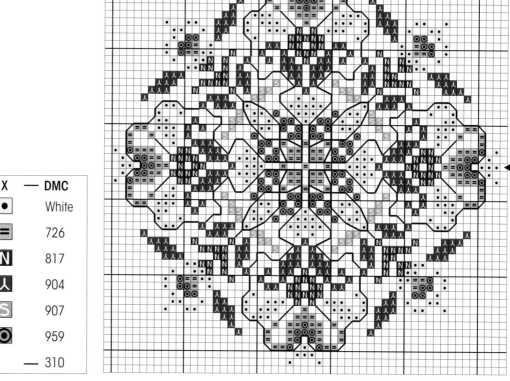

| X | — | DMC |
|---|---|---|
| ● | | White |
| = | | 726 |
| N | | 817 |
| 人 | | 904 |
| S | | 907 |
| ◉ | | 959 |
| — | | 310 |

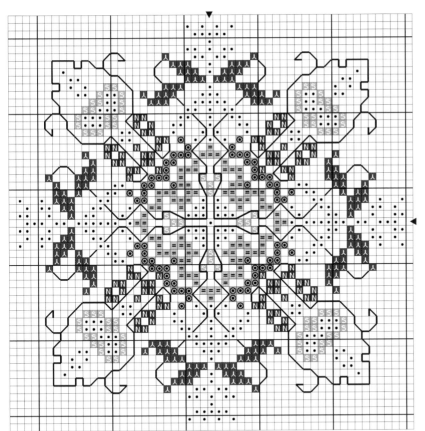

# Texas

The word "Texas" comes from the Spanish pronunciation, "tejas," of the Caddo word for friend or ally, and Texas is known as the Friendship State. It is also the largest state in the contiguous United States and the second most populous, with more than thirty million inhabitants!

I drew a lot of little mandalas that reminded me of dreamcatchers. What could be more natural for the land of western aspirations?

Bright navy blue has a positive meaning: order, exuberance, respect, uprightness, law, and justice. In spirituality, the color blue is associated with the fifth chakra, the throat chakra. This chakra, called Vishuddha, signifies purification.

ASSOCIATED STONE

## Sodalite

### *Benefits*

*Mental*

✳ Calms excessive emotions.

✳ Facilitates good elocution.

✳ Helps concentration and intellectual work.

✳ Soothes phobias and panic attacks.

✳ Promotes self-confidence and self-understanding.

✳ Develops solidarity and altruism.

✳ Helps counter feelings of inferiority.

*Physical*

✳ Balances blood pressure.

✳ Regulates the endocrine system.

✳ Promotes sleep in young children.

✳ Stimulates and energizes the nervous system.

✳ Soothes digestive system disorders.

✳ Increases general vitality.

✳ Helps fight diabetes.

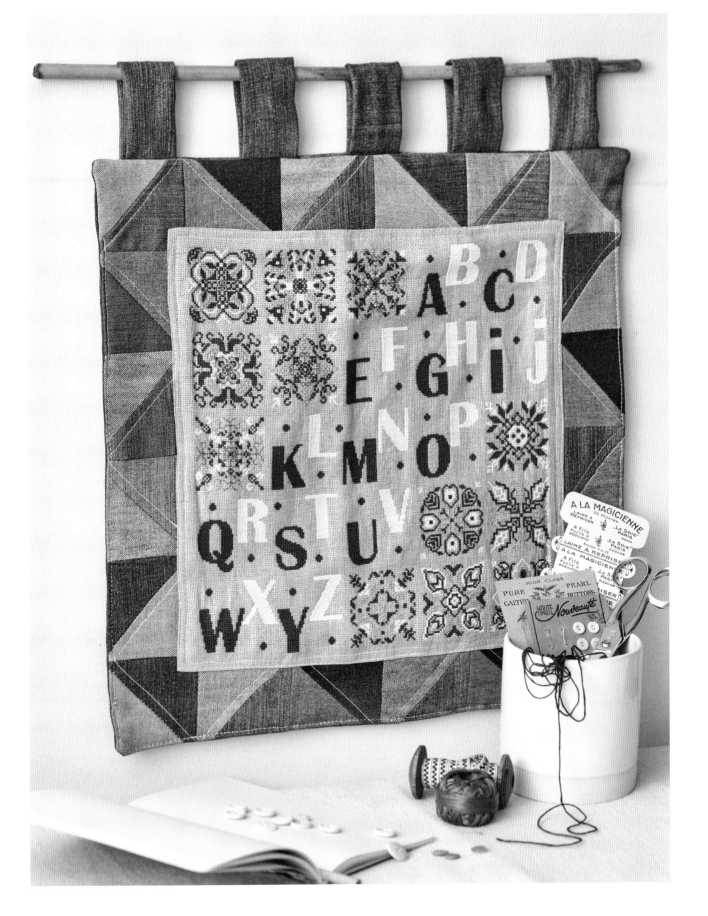

# Texas

## DIMENSIONS

Stitch count: 220 x 220
12.4 x 12.4 in. (31.4 x 31.4 cm)

## SUPPLIES

• Zweigart 18-count Linen Aida fabric (ref. 3419, color 53) (7 sts/cm)
• DMC Mouliné embroidery floss: 797, 809, 3801, 3865

## INSTRUCTIONS

Center the pattern on the fabric and cross-stitch using 2 strands of embroidery floss and backstitch using 1 strand of embroidery floss.

## CHART LAYOUT

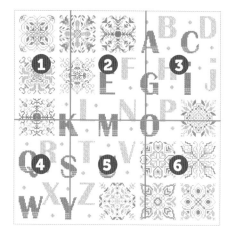

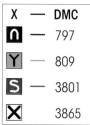

| X | — | DMC |
|---|---|-----|
| n | — | 797 |
| Y | — | 809 |
| S | — | 3801 |
| X | — | 3865 |

3

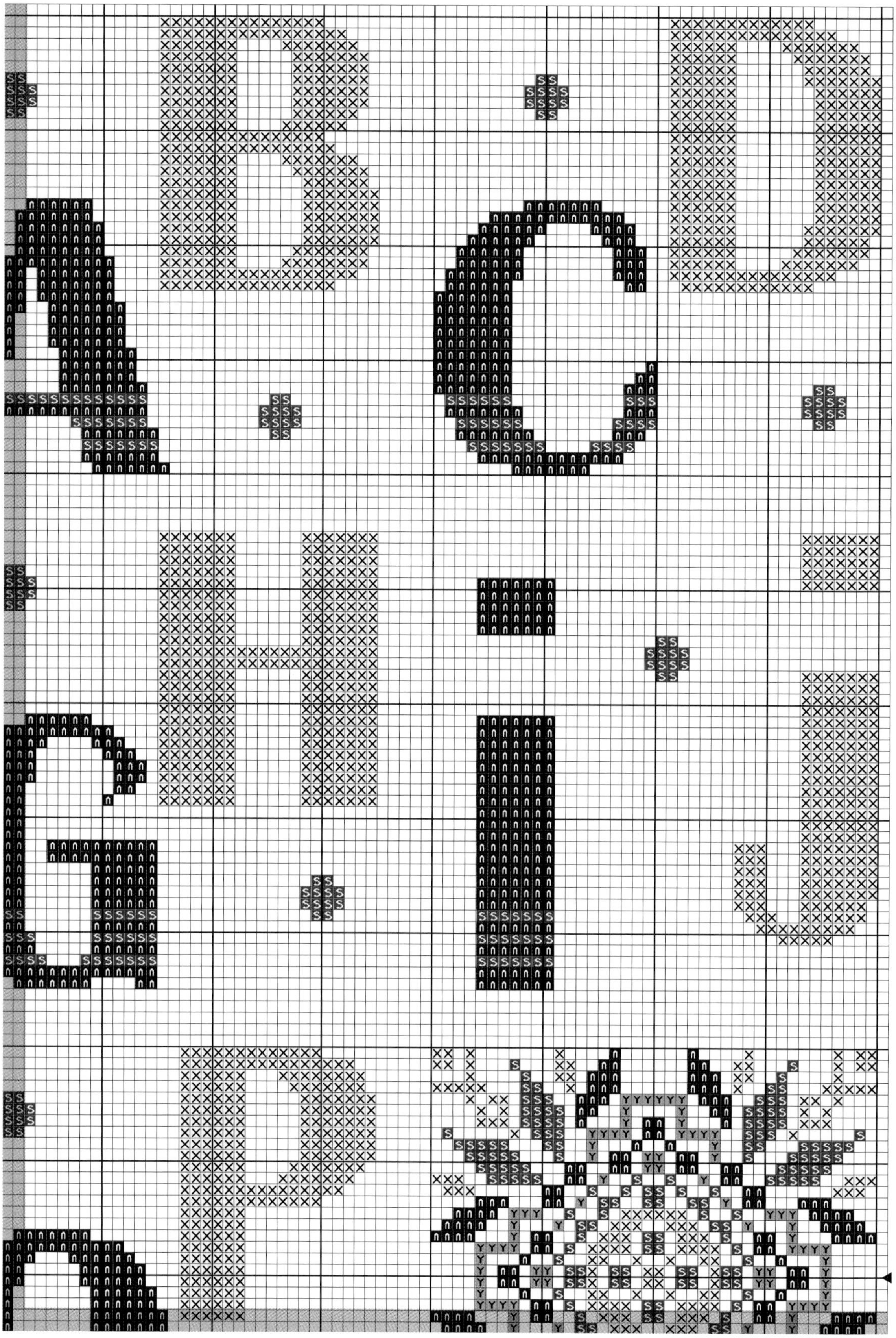

**4**

| X | — | DMC |
|---|---|---|
| n | — | 797 |
| Y | — | 809 |
| S | — | 3801 |
| X | — | 3865 |

# Kuala Lumpur

**K**uala Lumpur, often just called KL, the capital of Malaysia, is constantly expanding. Its city center still retains its human-scale neighborhoods. You will still come across monuments from the colonial era, with bits of Moorish or Mughal style. Kuala Lumpur is a charming, multiracial city, where very different ethnic groups live together.

Slightly outdated, old-fashioned storefronts line the streets of Chinatown and Little India in the heart of the city, where a breeze blows, heavy with incense from Chinese temples.

This design was inspired by the Holi Festival of Colors. My work felt very unsettled by all these colors, with an inability to make one stand out more than another. I let myself go in this whirlwind of color, and this design gave me a lot of inner joy and peace and lifted my spirits.

As I look at it, I remember the power that yellow brings to any mandala. This color is often seen as a symbol of wealth, but it is also associated with a deeper spirituality, particularly in Buddhist teachings.

ASSOCIATED STONE

## Baltic Amber

### *Benefits*

#### *Mental*

✳ Helps to find one's place and increase self-confidence.

✳ Purifies energies.

✳ Promotes intellectual development and creativity.

✳ Combats stress and depression.

#### *Physical*

✳ Treats skin problems such as acne, eczema, itching, and rashes.

✳ Promotes sleep and relieves migraines.

✳ Combats fatigue.

✳ Strengthens the immune system.

✳ Soothes muscular pain.

✳ Revives blood circulation.

✳ Soothes dental pain.

✳ Combats congestion of the respiratory tract.

# Kuala Lumpur

## DIMENSIONS

Stitch count: 225 x 225
14 x 14 in. (35.7 x 35.7 cm)

## SUPPLIES

- Thieffry Frères 32-count Wine linen (12 thr/cm)
- DMC Mouliné embroidery floss: white, 605, 666, 740, 743, 905, 907, 3804, 3846

| X | DMC |
|---|-----|
| ● | White |
| Y | 605 |
| S | 666 |
| Ɛ | 740 |
| C | 743 |
| Z | 905 |
| ◎ | 907 |
| ▼ | 3804 |
| ✚ | 3846 |

## INSTRUCTIONS

Center the pattern on the fabric and
cross-stitch using 2 strands of floss
over 2 threads of the fabric.

# Kuala Lumpur

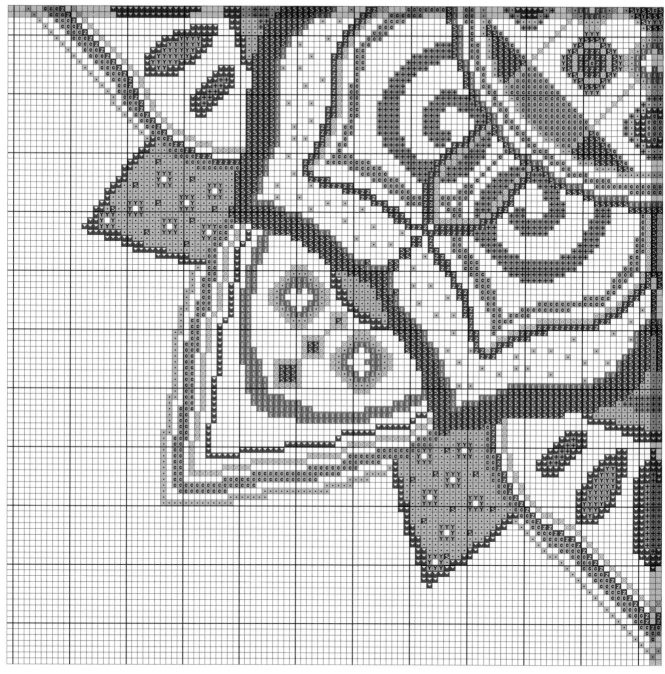

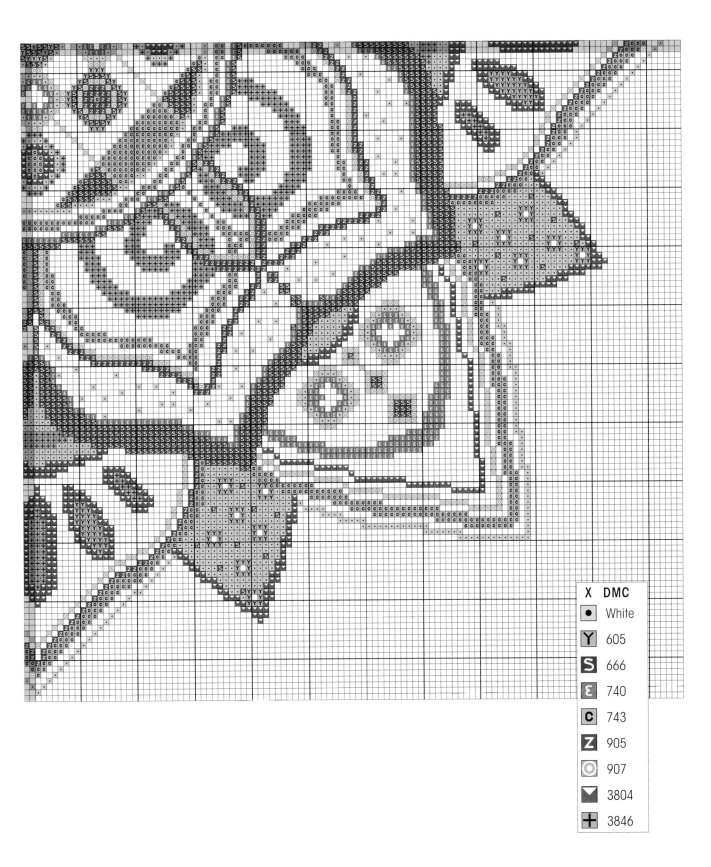

| X | DMC |
|---|-----|
| • | White |
| Y | 605 |
| S | 666 |
| ε | 740 |
| C | 743 |
| Z | 905 |
| ○ | 907 |
| ▼ | 3804 |
| + | 3846 |

# Belfast

There is a lot I could say about Ireland because I dream of going there, though so far I have only seen and discovered it through documentaries or other movies. The wild green landscapes, the old stones, and the special soul of Ireland are things I connect with intensely.

Belfast, the capital of Northern Ireland, is also the site of the naval shipyard where the famous RMS *Titanic* was built. The ship crashed into an iceberg before sinking on April 15 (my birthday), 1912. The city has a long history of religious division and political conflict, but today it is enjoying a time of peace and rebirth.

The dominant color is green! But not just any green; Irish green is special, and it is from this beautiful background that my design was born. Green is a symbol of nature, optimism, hope, and growth. It is also the color of the gardener and of hospitality. A good gardener is said to have a green thumb.

In a negative context, green can represent misfortune. A pale green shade changes the meaning of green into something more negative. It is a sign of degradation.

ASSOCIATED STONE

## Green Aventurine

### *Benefits*

*Mental*

* Transmits soothing, protective energy.
* Promotes tranquility and clarity of mind.
* Soothes fears and anxieties (especially in children).
* Absorbs harmful waves, including electromagnetic waves.

*Physical*

* Recommended for heart conditions and for circulatory and arterial disorders.
* Combats high cholesterol levels.
* Helps resolve skin problems such as eczema and psoriasis.

# Belfast

## DIMENSIONS

Stitch count: 87 x 260
5.4 x 16.2 in. (13.8 x 41.2 cm)

## SUPPLIES

- Thieffry Frères 32-count Almond Green linen (12 thr/cm)
- DMC Mouliné embroidery floss: white, 352, 725, 817, 827, 907, 3799

## INSTRUCTIONS

Center the pattern on the fabric and cross-stitch using 2 strands of floss over 2 threads of the fabric.

*Gold floss can be used in place of the yellow floss.*

| X | DMC |
|---|---|
| • | White |
| N | 352 |
| ◎ | 725 |
| S | 817 |
| ⋒ | 827 |
| 人 | 907 |
| ♥ | 3799 |

| X | DMC | |
|---|---|---|
| • | White | |
| N | 352 | |
| ⊙ | 725 | |
| S | 817 | |
| ∩ | 827 | |
| 人 | 907 | |
| ♥ | 3799 | |

# Ibiza

Ibiza is one of the islands in the Balearic archipelago in the Mediterranean. It is very famous for its lively nightlife downtown and in Sant Antoni, where Europe's leading nightclubs broadcast live in the summer.

When coming up with my design, I thought of Ibiza's colorful, festive day-to-night scene and had the idea of making a tote bag for the shopping queen that I am or two pillows to rest on after some crazy nights.

My Ibiza design is deliberately square, but like all mandalas, its strength lies in its center! So . . . let the party begin! The main color is bright red, which can represent contradictory emotions such as love and hate, life and death. It also symbolizes passion, temptation, perseverance, energy, the forbidden, anger, and determination. Red stimulates our physical senses and the deep passions between us, such as sex, love, hatred, and revenge. Red excites our emotions, spurring us to action and alerting us to danger. In feng shui, the brighter the red is, the more it energizes our surroundings.

ASSOCIATED STONE

## Carnelian

### *Benefits*

#### Mental

✳ Symbolizes vitality and courage.

✳ Has beneficial healing properties due to its warm, vivid hue.

✳ Brings a good mood and self-confidence.

✳ Makes you love life and encourages creativity.

✳ Calms anger and resenment, despite its "all fire, all flame" side.

✳ Encourages patience and even, if necessary, resignation.

#### Physical

✳ Believed to stop hemorrhages and accelerate healing with astringent properties.

✳ Relieves stomachaches of all kinds as well as rheumatic and lumbar pain.

# Ibiza

## DIMENSIONS

Stitch count: 151 x 151 (each square)
11.9 x 11.9 in. (30.2 x 30.2 cm)

## SUPPLIES

• Zweigart 25-count Red Lugana evenweave (ref. 3835, color 954) (10 thr/cm)

• Zweigart 25-count Vanilla Lugana evenweave (ref. 3835, color 274) (10 thr/cm)

• DMC Mouliné embroidery floss:
Red side: white, 725, 741, 904, 907, 995
Vanilla side: white, 666, 797, 813, 827, 907

## INSTRUCTIONS

Center each pattern on the appropriate fabric and cross-stitch using 2 strands of floss over 2 threads of the fabric.

Only ¼ of each pattern is shown. Transfer 4 times, rotating 90° for each quarter.

*Embroidered fabric made into tote bag by designer Delphine Vasseur ("Takalfaire," couleurs-cabanes.fr)*

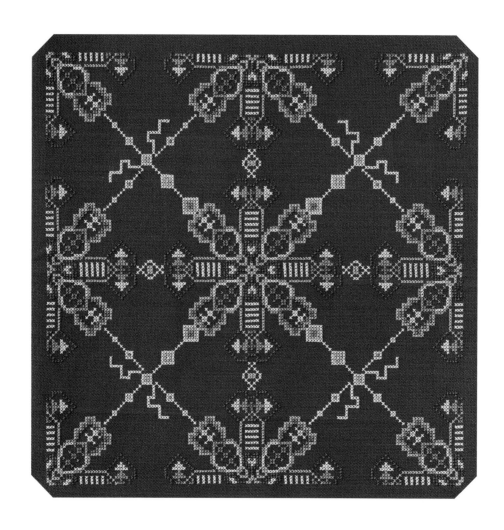

Motif A

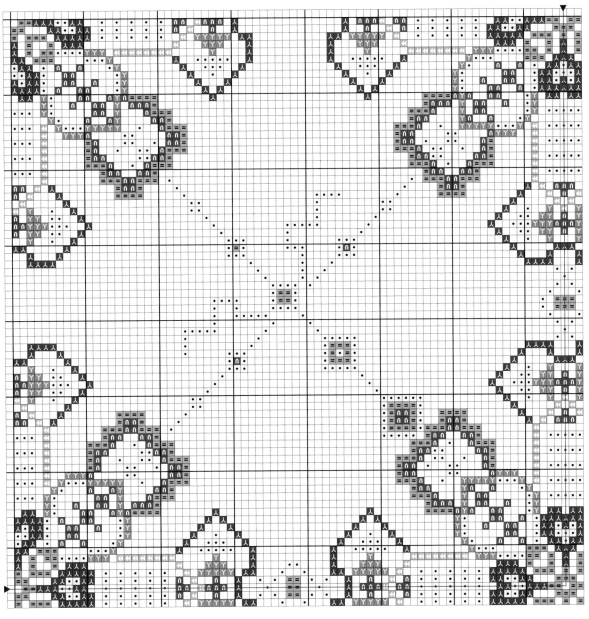

| X | DMC |
|---|---|
| ● | White |
| = | 725 |
| Y | 741 |
| 人 | 904 |
| ≪ | 907 |
| ∩ | 995 |

Motif B

| X | DMC | |
|---|---|---|
| ● | White | |
| S | 666 | |
| N | 797 | |
| C | 813 | |
| Y | 827 | |
| ◀ | 907 | |

# Romania

**R**omania is a country in southeastern Europe known for its forest region of Transylvania, surrounded by the Carpathian Mountains. Its capital, Bucharest, commonly known as "Little Paris" because of its palaces and beautiful buildings from the early twentieth century, is an elegant and majestic city.

Romanian embroidery, frequently found on traditional folk garments, closely resembles Ukrainian and Eastern embroideries, recognizable by their bright red, black, and sometimes blue colors.

In European civilizations, each of these colors has a specific meaning. Black is primarily associated with mourning, death, the absence of light, and even fear. But in color psychology, it suggests discipline and power, as well as sophistication and success. In feng shui, it is a powerful color synonymous with respect. It also represents money and power.

ASSOCIATED STONE

## Black Obsidian

### *Benefits*

#### *Mental*

✳ Brings calm and balance.

✳ Promotes meditation as well as inner peace and clarity of mind.

✳ Helps to shed light and overcome past wounds; known as the "stone of truth."

#### *Physical*

✳ Calms pain, cramps, nausea, irritation, and allergies.

✳ Helps healing.

✳ Fortifies the body in general.

✳ Helps absorb harmful waves and pollution when placed in a living space.

# Romania

## DIMENSIONS

Stitch count: 123 x 123
7.7 x 7.7 in. (19.5 x 19.5 cm)

## SUPPLIES

• Zweigart 32-count Natural Belfast linen (ref. 3609, color 53) (12 thr/cm)
• DMC Mouliné embroidery floss: 310, 321, 995, 3865

## INSTRUCTIONS

Center the pattern on the fabric and cross-stitch using 2 strands of floss and backstitch using 1 strand of embroidery floss over 2 threads of the fabric.

*The pattern is inserted in a round tray made from an exotic wood.*

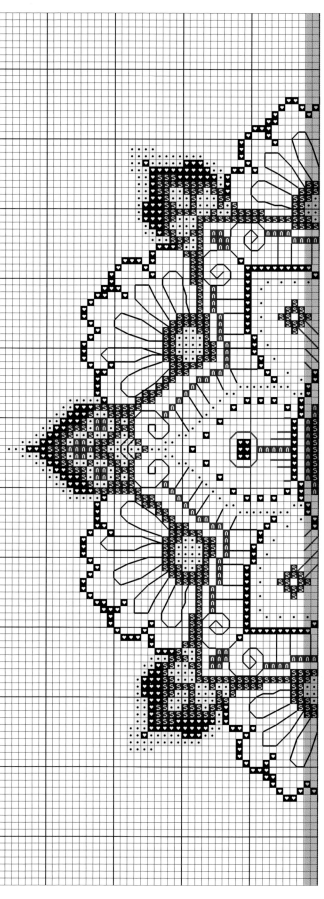

| X | — | DMC |
|---|---|---|
| ♥ | — | 310 |
| S | | 321 |
| n | — | 995 |
| • | | 3865 |

75

# France

I had to make a stopover in my own country, France, because traveling elsewhere with my designs is great, but returning home and settling in is also restful.

I chose to draw parts of mandalas. In France, the mandala craze has been around for years—first in schools to help children to discover colors, but also to create psychological support for young and old alike.

I have embroidered words that fit me and ones with which the word "mandala" is very often associated. The letters are not in black but dark brown. Brown is a symbol of raw strength, also associated with wood and leather, and can inspire stability. And for those with a sweet tooth, it is also the color of chocolate! This warm, earthy color goes perfectly with travel and cultural discovery.

ASSOCIATED STONE

## Bull's Eye

Bull's Eye quartz has all the characteristics of Tiger's Eye.

### *Benefits*

#### *Mental*

✳ Repels bad intentions and wards off harmful waves as a stone of anchoring and protection.

✳ Strengthens courage, stamina, and mental strength.

✳ Allows us to assert ourselves while remaining anchored in the reality around us.

✳ Encourages action, decision-making, and autonomy.

#### *Physical*

✳ Improves reflexes and promotes the practice of all sports.

✳ Strengthens bones, teeth, and nails and supports night vision.

✳ Transmits boundless energy; its stimulating effects boost libido, restore vitality and dynamism, and accelerate metabolism in general.

# France

## DIMENSIONS

Stitch count: 208 x 138
13 x 8.7 in. (33 x 22 cm)

## SUPPLIES

• Zweigart 32-count Off-white Murano evenweave
(ref. 3984, color 101) (12 thr/cm)
• DMC Mouliné embroidery floss:
600, 725, 3371, 3819, 3844

## INSTRUCTIONS

Center the pattern on the fabric and cross-stitch
using 2 strands of floss and backstitch using 1
strand of floss over 2 threads of the fabric.

## CHART LAYOUT

**①**

| X | — | DMC |
|---|---|------|
| S | | 600 |
| X | | 725 |
| ε | — | 3371 |
| U | | 3819 |
| ◀ | — | 3844 |

**3**

**❹**

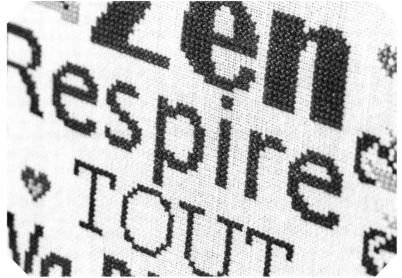

| X | — | DMC |
|---|---|---|
| S | | 600 |
| X | | 725 |
| Ɛ | — | 3371 |
| U | | 3819 |
| ◄ | — | 3844 |

# Casablanca

Casablanca is a port city and commercial hub in western Morocco, along the Atlantic Ocean.

As far as I'm concerned, the hand of Fatima has soothing power. I lost one given to me by a Moroccan school friend, which I had received as a good-luck charm and token of friendship. It goes by many different names. It is called the hamsa in reference to the number five and the five fingers of the hand it represents. Muslims also call it the hand of Fatima or Fatima's hand, referring to Fatima, the Prophet Muhammad's daughter. Jews call it Miriam's hand, in reference to Moses's sister and prophetess. Moroccan door knockers are often in the shape of a hamsa to protect the house.

I love this hand and wanted the pattern to be on a large scale. I can't explain it, but this symbol resonates deep inside of me. It is everywhere, all over the place: in decorative elements, on doors, and in jewelry, of course. It is the ultimate good-luck token to protect against the evil eye and ward off evil intentions. The hand can be worn or displayed facing either up or down.

Orange, often associated with communication and creativity, is a warm color that inspires and brings a good mood. Along with yellow, it well represents the traits of vigor and open-mindedness.

ASSOCIATED STONE

## Sunstone (Heliolite)

### Benefits

#### Mental

✳ Combats the sad feelings that often overshadow our daily lives, like worry, anxiety, and depression.

✳ Helps us appreciate life and encourages creativity and all forms of artistic and physical expression.

✳ Affirms willpower and self-confidence.

✳ Brings a positive attitude.

#### Physical

✳ Combats a lack of tone often found during the winter months.

✳ Relieves all forms of seasonal allergies as well as persistent sore throats and gastric problems.

# Casablanca

## DIMENSIONS

Stitch count: 183 x 241
11.4 x 15 in. (29 x 38.2 cm)

## SUPPLIES

- Thieffry Frères 32-count Saffron linen (12 thr/cm)
- DMC Mouliné embroidery floss: white, 310, 349, 744, 3765, 3766, 3844

## INSTRUCTIONS

Center the pattern on the fabric and cross-stitch using 2 strands of floss and backstitch using 1 strand of floss over 2 threads of the fabric.

| X | — | DMC |
|---|---|---|
| • | — | White |
| ♥ | | 310 |
| S | | 349 |
| Y | | 744 |
| ▼ | | 3765 |
| N | | 3766 |
| ∩ | | 3844 |

# Papeete

This is a dream destination that for many remains only a dream, but I'm glad that my mind wandered there anyway. I will likely never go there, so I am bringing you my colors and mandalas as I see them when I close my eyes.

Papeete, on the island of Tahiti, is the capital of French Polynesia, a group of islands in the South Pacific. It is a port on the west coast of the island of Tahiti, which is famous for its rare black pearls.

Fuchsia symbolizes devotion, compatibility, union, love, and affection. This shade of pink nourishes, heals, and protects on an emotional level. Fuchsia is a mixture of deep pink and blue; it inspires confidence and maturity, a more responsible and controlled love.

ASSOCIATED STONE

## Rose Quartz

### *Benefits*

*Mental*

* Promotes calm, inner peace, serenity, and tranquility.

* Heals emotional wounds.

* Calms episodes of anxiety.

* Soothes jealousy and heartache.

* Alleviates lack of confidence and restores self-esteem.

* Dispels nightmares.

*Physical*

* Relieves migraines and headaches.

* Regulates blood circulation and blood pressure.

* Promotes falling asleep and experiencing restorative sleep.

* Provides support to overcome depression.

* Helps healing of wounds and general convalescence.

Rose quartz is not only the stone of the heart but also the stone of artists.
It aids understanding of art and provides support in the creative process.
Artists are advised to place it on their desk or in their studio.

# Papeete

## DIMENSIONS

Stitch count: 92 x 288
7.2 x 22.7 in. (18.4 x 57.6 cm)

## SUPPLIES

• Zweigart 25-count Bright Aqua Lugana cotton evenweave (ref. 3835, color 5142) (10 thr/cm)
• DMC Mouliné embroidery floss: white, 209, 211, 310, 349, 725, 741, 820, 827, 904, 906, 907, 995, 3804, 3846

## INSTRUCTIONS

Center the pattern on the fabric and cross-stitch using 2 strands of floss over 2 threads of the fabric.

*Embroidered fabric made into a banner by designer Delphine Vasseur ("Takalfaire," couleurs-cabanes.fr)*

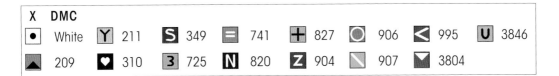

| X | DMC | | | | | | | |
|---|---|---|---|---|---|---|---|---|
| ● White | Y 211 | S 349 | = 741 | + 827 | ◉ 906 | ◄ 995 | U 3846 |
| ▲ 209 | ♥ 310 | 3 725 | N 820 | Z 904 | ◢ 907 | ▼ 3804 | |

# Finland

I subconsciously returned to Finland after designing the Helsinki pattern. I surprised myself by creating this more structured design, one much further away from its capital, and which I think recalls the magnificent designs of sweaters, socks, and mittens created in this country. Finland is vast. It is a northern European nation bordering Sweden, Norway, and Russia.

The bright green color is invigorating and refreshing. It is a color with calming properties that brings harmony or balance. It is a symbol of eternity and rebirth, as well as of authority ("green lights," literally and figuratively).

ASSOCIATED STONE

## Nephrite Jade

### *Benefits*

*Mental*

✳ Delivers a message of harmony and serenity.

✳ Stimulates intuition and sheds new light on our inner reflections.

✳ Embodies luck and happiness.

*Physical*

✳ Promotes the elimination of kidney stones and contributes to the proper functioning of the adrenal glands, sometimes responsible for high blood pressure. Traditionally used specifically for the treatment of kidney disorder.

✳ Acts effectively on urinary disorders such as cystitis, incontinence, and enuresis.

*A thought to my little girl, who bears this wonderful name.*

# Finland

## DIMENSIONS

Stitch count: 42 x 42 (one square)
3 x 3 in. (7.6 x 7.6 cm)

## SUPPLIES

• Zweigart 27-count Black Linda evenweave
(ref. 1235, color 720) (11 thr/cm)
• DMC Mouliné embroidery floss: white,
321, 725, 904, 907

## INSTRUCTIONS

Center the pattern on the fabric and
cross-stitch using 2 strands of floss
over 2 threads of the fabric.

*Raw wood embroidery floss organizers
and wood stand created by
Auvergne Laser, www.al63.fr.*

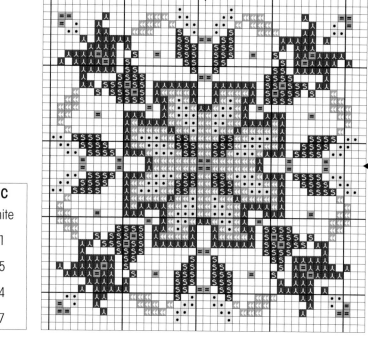

| X | DMC |
|---|---|
| ● | White |
| S | 321 |
| = | 725 |
| 人 | 904 |
| ◀ | 907 |

# Delft

**D**elft, a town on the western edge of the Netherlands, is widely known as the cradle of the blue and white pottery bearing its name: Delftware or Delft pottery!

I was lucky enough to visit it with my friend Bernadette, who used to live in the Netherlands, and to thus discover the magnificent blue color of this famous earthenware. Delft is also world-renowned for its porcelain, Johannes Vermeer, and the Royal House, as well as for its marvelous canals.

Generally associated with calm and stability, the color blue also represents trust, loyalty, or truth. Blue is also closely linked to well-being and spirituality. It is often associated with serenity, wisdom, and dreams. Omnipresent in our lives, blue is synonymous with escape and is a symbol of loyalty, justice, and faith. For the Egyptians, blue was a lucky color linked to immortality and truth.

ASSOCIATED STONE

## Lapis Lazuli

### *Benefits*

#### *Mental*

✳ Helps one overcome life's trials and regain serenity.

✳ Facilitates communication and encourages sociability, particularly helpful for shy temperaments.

✳ Develops creative expression and brings thoroughness and concentration.

✳ Stimulates intuition and the understanding of dreams through its deep color.

#### *Physical*

✳ Treats aches and pains, especially migraines and other headaches.

✳ Soothes burns and skin eruptions of allergic origin such as eczema or urticaria. Dermatology is a special field for this stone.

✳ Soothes eye and ear disorders.

Regularly wearing a donut-shaped lapis lazuli stone around the neck protects against minor winter ailments that affect the throat and chest (sore throats, coughs).

# Delft

## DIMENSIONS

Stitch count: 164 x 164
10.2 x 10.2 in. (26 x 26 cm)

## SUPPLIES

• Zweigart 32-count Off-white Murano evenweave (ref. 3984, color 101) (12 thr/cm)
• DMC Mouliné embroidery floss: 796, 798, 799, 3325

## INSTRUCTIONS

Center the pattern on the fabric. Cross-stitch using 2 strands of floss and backstitch using 1 strand of floss over 2 threads of the fabric.

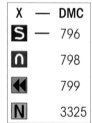

| X | — | DMC |
|---|---|---|
| S | — | 796 |
| n | | 798 |
| ◀ | | 799 |
| N | | 3325 |

# Delft

| X | — | DMC |
|---|---|---|
| S | — | 796 |
| n | | 798 |
| ◀◀ | | 799 |
| N | | 3325 |

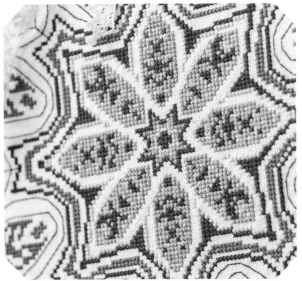

103

# Kharkiv

I started this project a year ago with the Moscow pattern. Kharkiv ended up being the natural conclusion to this book, so that the symbolism of peace represented by this mandala can do its work, at least in my heart.

Kharkiv, or Kharkov, is the second-largest city in Ukraine. It is one of that country's most dynamic cultural and academic centers. In addition to its university, founded in 1805, it boasts a host of other higher education establishments (polytechnic institute, university of medicine and agriculture, engineering schools). It is also the location of several scientific research facilities, a sports center, botanical gardens, as well as a philharmonic concert hall, theaters (the oldest dates back to 1780), a planetarium, and numerous museums.

I have connected the color white to this mandala, primarily as the symbol of peace. While in Western countries white is associated with purity and peace and is a symbol of wisdom and innocence, in Asia it is the color of mourning.

The primary significance of the color white is spiritual. Associated with light, the color white is both a sign of the divine and an expression of the highest moral values. One can legitimately question the value of the color white. It all depends on one's point of view. In physics, white is not categorized as a color.

ASSOCIATED STONE

## Moonstone

### *Benefits*

#### *Mental*

* Brings calm and serenity.

* Calms anxieties and protects from stress.

* Soothes angry and rigid natures, giving them the gentleness they need.

* Helps create and maintain relationships that are gentle and harmonious.

* Helps stimulate creative power.

* Inspires clairvoyance and premonition and fosters lucid dreams.

#### *Physical*

* Balances hormonal systems and, consequently, reduces acne.

* Brings calm to hyperactive children.

* Relieves insect bites.

* Controls thyroid function.

* Calms related digestive disorders and reduces them during periods of stress.

* Soothes disorders associated with menstruation and menopause, promotes fertility, protects during pregnancy and childbirth, and stimulates lactation.

Moonstone is, above all, a feminine stone.

# Kharkiv

## DIMENSIONS

Stitch count: 285 x 285
17.8 x 17.8 in. (45.2 x 45.2 cm)

## SUPPLIES

• Zweigart 32-count Natural Belfast linen (ref. 3609, color 53)

• DMC Mouliné embroidery floss: white, 310, 321; Diamant Metallic D3852

## INSTRUCTIONS

Center the pattern on the fabric and cross-stitch using 2 strands of floss over 2 threads of the fabric.

## CHART LAYOUT

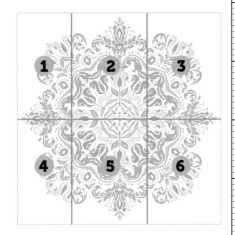

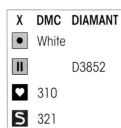

| X | DMC | DIAMANT |
|---|-----|---------|
| • | White | |
| ‖ | | D3852 |
| ♥ | 310 | |
| S | 321 | |

| X | DMC | DIAMANT |
|---|---|---|
| • | White | |
| II | | D3852 |
| ♥ | 310 | |
| S | 321 | |

| X | DMC | DIAMANT |
|---|-----|---------|
| ● | White | |
| ‖ | | D3852 |
| ♥ | 310 | |
| S | 321 | |

# Acknowledgments

Thanks to Viviane Rousset and her team at Éditions de Saxe for their confidence in me.

**To you, Jean-Michel**, a particular and somewhat mystical part of my personality that you probably didn't know existed, and yet I believe in all this soft magic.

To my four children: to **Julien**, **Aurélien**, **Alexandre**, this particular year has made me realize how much mandalas and the study of colors and stones was important to help bear the sorrows we shared, and to **Lola**, my teenager, to whom I'm going to offer all the stones explained in this book to help her get through the difficult period of adolescence. The four of you are the center of all my life interests and my inner light.

To my two granddaughters with all my love: **Jade** and **Élise**, I'll take the time to draw you your own mandalas and choose your lucky stones with you.

To my parents, **Cosette** and **Roger**, and my father-in-law, **Marc**: thank you for always being there by my side.

To my stars, up there, my pain, my light, my strength.

A huge thanks to all the hands who helped with this book: Laurence Destribats, Dominique Roubault, Sylvie Petagna, Frédérique Ville, Noëlle Proust, Patricia Mandin, Martine Dimicolis, Florence François, Germaine Aubert, and Thérèse Baux.

Thanks to my "Cabane" friends, Séverine and Delphine, for their professionalism, and to Tiane, the fun seamstress.

Thank you to my cross-stitch friends from all the fairs, exhibitions, and Facebook, and to those who pass through and come back to the "Cabane" every year.

To all of you who have this book in your hands, I send you lots of light and good cheer. It is up to you to choose the colors that suit you best to give you much joy embroidering the patterns in this book.

Happy zen cross-stitching.

**Isabelle Haccourt Vautier**

P.S. If, like me, you love crystal healing, I recommend the book *The Crystal Healer* by Philip Permutt.

## STACKPOLE BOOKS

An imprint of The Globe Pequot Publishing Group, Inc.
64 South Main Street
Essex, CT 06426
www.globepequot.com

Distributed by NATIONAL BOOK NETWORK
800-462-6420

Original title: *Les mandalas brodés au point de croix*
© *Les éditions de saxe* 2022

Designer: Isabelle Haccourt Vautier
Layout: Evelyne Nobre
Photos: Richard Boutin
Styling: Vania Leroy

*All rights reserved.* No part of this book may be reproduced in any form or by any electronic or mechanical means, including information storage and retrieval systems, without written permission from the publisher, except by a reviewer who may quote passages in a review.

The contents of this book are for personal use only. Patterns herein may be reproduced in limited quantities for such use. Any large-scale commercial reproduction is prohibited without the written consent of the publisher.

We have made every effort to ensure the accuracy and completeness of these instructions. We cannot, however, be responsible for human error, typographical mistakes, or variations in individual work.

British Library Cataloguing in Publication Information available

Library of Congress Cataloging-in-Publication Data is available

ISBN 9780811776837 (paperback) | ISBN 9780811776844 (ebook)

♾™ The paper used in this publication meets the minimum requirements of American National Standard for Information Sciences—Permanence of Paper for Printed Library Materials, ANSI/NISO Z39.48-1992.